11/99

Affirmative Action

A Problem

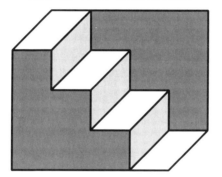

or a Remedy?

JoAnn Bren Guernsey

LERNER PUBLICATIONS COMPANY • MINNEAPOLIS

Library of Congress Cataloging-in-Publication Data

Guernsey, JoAnn Bren.
   Affirmative action : A Problem or a Remedy? / JoAnn Bren Guernsey.
     p. cm.
   Includes bibliographical references and index.
   Summary: Discusses the pros and cons of affirmative action policy
in this country, examining its history, its effects, and current
problems, including the question of reverse discrimination.
   ISBN 0-8225-2614-X (alk. paper)
   1. Affirmative action programs—United States—Juvenile
literature. 2. Race discrimination—United States—Juvenile
literature. 3. Reverse discrimination—United States—Juvenile
literature. [1. Affirmative action programs. 2. Race
discrimination. 3. Reverse discrimination. 4. Discrimination.]
I. Title.
HF5549.5.A34G84 1997   97-1087
331.13'3'0973—dc21

Manufactured in the United States of America
1 2 3 4 5 6 – JR – 02 01 00 99 98 97

CONTENTS

FOREWORD

If a nation expects to be ignorant and free, . . . it expects what never was and never will be.

Thomas Jefferson

Are you ready to participate in forming the policies of our government? Many issues are very confusing, and it can be difficult to know what to think about them or how to make a decision about them. Sometimes you must gather information about a subject before you can be informed enough to make a decision. Bernard Baruch, a prosperous American financier and an advisor to every president from Woodrow Wilson to Dwight D. Eisenhower, said, "If you can get all the facts, your judgment can be right; if you don't get all the facts, it can't be right."

But gathering information is only one part of the decision-making process. The way you interpret information is influenced by the values you have been taught since infancy—ideas about right and wrong, good and bad. Many of your values are shaped, or at least influenced, by how and where you grow up, by your race, sex, and religion, by how much money your family has. What your parents believe, what they read, and what you read and believe influence your decisions. The values of friends and teachers also affect what you think.

It's always good to listen to the opinions of people around you, but you will often confront contradictory points of view and points of view that are based not on fact, but on myth. John F. Kennedy, the 35th president of the United States, said, "The great enemy of the truth is very often not the lie—deliberate, contrived, and dishonest—but the myth—persistent, persuasive, and unrealistic." Eventually you will have to separate fact from myth and make up your own mind, make your own decisions. Because you are responsible for your decisions, it's important to get as much information as you can. Then your decisions will be the right ones for you.

Making a fair and informed decision can be an exciting process, a chance to examine new ideas and different points of view. You live in a world that changes quickly and sometimes dramatically—a world that offers the opportunity to explore the ever-changing ground between yourself and others. Instead of forming a single, easy, or popular point of view, you might develop a rich and complex vision that offers new alternatives. Explore the many dimensions of an idea. Find kinship among an extensive range of opinions. Only after you've done this should you try to form your own opinions.

After you have formed an opinion about a particular subject, you may believe it is the only right decision. But some people will disagree with you and challenge your beliefs. They are not trying to antagonize you or put you down. They probably believe that they're right as sincerely as you believe you are. Thomas Macaulay, an English historian and author, wrote, "Men are never so likely to settle a question rightly as when they discuss it freely." In a democracy, the free exchange of ideas is not only encouraged, it's vital. Examining and discussing public issues and understanding opposing ideas are desirable and necessary elements of a free nation's ability to govern itself.

The Pro/Con series is designed to explore and examine different points of view on contemporary issues and to help you develop an understanding and appreciation of them. Most importantly, it will help you form your own opinions and make your own honest, informed decision.

Mary Winget
Series Editor

Should colleges consider race and sex when selecting students for admission, or should grades and test scores be the only determining factors?

WHAT IS AFFIRMATIVE ACTION?

When three high school seniors in a Midwestern town decided to apply for college admission, they all set their sights on the same prestigious Ivy League school. Rob achieved a GPA (grade point average) that put him in the top 10 percent of his class and his SAT (Scholastic Aptitude Test) scores were excellent. Julie's GPA and SAT scores were almost identical to Rob's. But Sam barely maintained average grades and his SAT scores were disappointing. Rob, who is white, was the only one of the three who was rejected by the college. Julie would join the growing but still small female population on campus; and Sam, who is African American and poor, was not only accepted but also offered enough scholarship money to attend the following fall.

Did the admissions office make a fair decision? Was the decision unfair but "okay" in this case? The college's administrators would defend their policies by saying that it was necessary to reach out to both females and minorities in order to make the student population more diverse and representative of society at large. Without this kind of help, Sam could have remained stuck in poverty with no chance of a college education. But with preferential treatment by the college, he has an opportunity for a bright future. Rob, it might be argued, will probably succeed in life no matter what college he attends.

If the American public were asked to voice opinions about what happened to these three students, the response would be sharply divided. Many people would cheer and say, "It's about time." But many others—men and women and members of all races—would be angry. Nobody would be particularly surprised, however, by this apparent discrimination against Rob. Colleges and employers have been making such difficult decisions for almost three decades, in the name of *affirmative action.* Affirmative action is a term used to describe techniques to remedy the effects of existing and past discrimination and to end such discrimination.

The original basis for affirmative action was the assumption that members of all racial groups should appear in all institutions and activities more or less in proportion to their numbers in the general population. The "underrepresentation" of any racial group, it was decided, was evidence of discrimination.[1] It wasn't long before this assumption included other minorities and women as well, because of the long history of *their* underrepresentation.

Defining affirmative action, however, is not a simple task. Harvard law professor Randall Kennedy defines it as "policies that provide preferences based explicitly on membership in a designated group."[2] But other people try to avoid using the term "preferences" because it can ignite any discussion of affirmative action into a fiery debate about who benefits from and who gets hurt by such policies. Affirmative action was not initially designed to punish or exclude anyone; it was an attempt to expand opportunity for *everybody*.[3] But its meaning has changed gradually and in subtle ways since the 1960s.

AN EXPLOSION OF CONTROVERSY

Affirmative action touches almost every area of American life, and conflict has often been the most visible result. In the workplace, affirmative action hiring programs can mean the difference between having a job or being unemployed, between living in comfort and struggling to survive. And it can make people like Peter Muus angry.

When Muus couldn't find a job, he became convinced it was because he was white. To test this theory, he applied for a mortgage clerk job at two branches of the same company in Minnesota. On two separate application forms, he answered all the questions the same except the one regarding race. Even though everything else about the "black" and the "white" Peter Muus was identical, only the "black" applicant was called for an interview.

Muus considers this treatment an example of reverse discrimination, and he's not alone in holding that position. But don't racial preferences represent a positive step toward equality in many cases? Consider a situation, for example, in which two equally qualified people—one white and one black—are seeking a teaching job. Without affirmative action, the position might be filled, in effect, by tossing a coin. Is that better than making a choice based on the idea that American schools (and black students) might benefit from having more black teachers?[4]

During the 1990s, especially, many middle-class and working-class white males found themselves sliding into poverty because of layoffs, lower wages, and reduced benefits. They pointed to affirmative action as

Many white males oppose affirmative action because they think it is a form of reverse discrimination.

one of the main causes of their predicament. Opportunities seemed to be denied them in order to open opportunities for women and minorities. Thus emerged what appeared to be a mass of "angry white males."

Not everyone, however, feels this anger is justified. Many experts believe that affirmative action has become a convenient scapegoat for a white middle class in crisis. Michael Kinsley, in his *New Yorker* article "The Spoils of Victimhood," questioned why whites have been "whipped into a fury of resentment over affirmative action."[5] While anxiety about the future is understandable (for all classes and races), the exact role of affirmative action in the financial and employment woes of whites is debatable. The percentage of blacks who are unemployed is still higher, after all, than white unemployment rates. And, as pointed out by Kinsley, "blacks still trail whites in every major prestige occupation outside sports."[6]

Furthermore, affirmative action is not the only form of preferential treatment; it's just the one that provokes the most protest. In businesses, preference is frequently shown to relatives or friends of the people in charge. Experts have been quick to point out that Henry Ford II, for instance, didn't run Ford Motor Company because he was the most qualified person for the job.[7]

Colleges and universities have been even more blatant in their long-standing preferential policies. Most prestigious colleges have admitted students—even with mediocre grades and test scores—simply because a parent or grandparent attended that college. And many colleges have routinely sought *geographic*

Colleges and universities—especially prestigious ones, such as the University of California at Berkeley—have used preferential policies to achieve diversity on campus.

diversity. They show preference to a student from a state that is underrepresented. A few rejected students may have grumbled about the unfairness of that situation, but the response to these preferential policies is nothing like the rage inspired by affirmative action.

Why? Because, most experts agree, the affirmative action issue involves race. Many universities and colleges have reported their student bodies becoming more and more split along racial lines, and officials are concerned about the dramatic increase in racial tension. The painting of a swastika and the words "white power" on Yale University's African-American cultural center in 1988 is only one of many disturbing examples of this tension.

The controversy over affirmative action policies does not exist only on college campuses and in the workplace, however. It affects everyone. Public opinion polls during the 1990s show how Americans feel about the issue. In 1995, a *Wall Street Journal*/NBC News poll found that two out of three Americans opposed affirmative action.[8] But when the polls were divided along racial lines, the results were more revealing. A 1995 *Newsweek* poll suggests that whites oppose racial preferences in employment or college admissions by a margin of 74 percent to 14 percent; minorities questioned supported these policies by a 50 to 46 percent margin.[9]

The language used in polls, however, makes a difference in the results. If just the term "affirmative action" is used in the poll, larger percentages support it. But if other terms are used, such as "preferences" or "quotas" (when a set number of places *must* be filled by members of a preferred group), the public objects more often and more loudly.[10] Similarly, public opinion is often determined by which group the affirmative action programs are designed to help. In the view held by many people, these programs should apply only to blacks to compensate them for the centuries of oppression and discrimination dating back to slavery. According to many others, however, women and ethnic minorities also should be included.[11]

Former Supreme Court justice Harry Blackmun supported affirmative action.

SUPPORT FOR AFFIRMATIVE ACTION

Many people who support affirmative action admit that it can cause serious resentment among those who don't qualify for group preferences, but allowing inequities to continue can also cause serious consequences. Isn't it unrealistic, supporters ask, to expect racism and sexism to disappear completely in only a few decades? Can America so easily and quickly become a "color-blind" and "gender-blind" society? Centuries of institutional discrimination make it all too natural for the biggest corporations and best colleges to draw on the groups they have always turned to, rather than reach out to others.

In defense of affirmative action, Supreme Court justice Harry Blackmun observed in 1978 that "in order to get beyond racism, we must first take account of race. There is no other way. And in order to treat some persons equally, we must treat them differently."[12]

Without question, progress against discrimination has been made. Affirmative action, up to a point, has benefited minorities (especially blacks) and women. It has allowed many people, in a relatively short period of time, to acquire college degrees, training, and jobs that would have been impossible in the past. Without affirmative action, for example, it's unlikely that blacks would account for 41 percent of all new police officers between 1970 and 1990, or that 1.3 million blacks would be working in government service.[13]

These graduates of the New York Police Academy show the diversity achieved by affirmative action policies.

In April 1996, Hendrik Hertzberg and Henry Louis Gates Jr. introduced a special issue of *The New Yorker* ("Black in America") by first pointing to many of the achievements of African Americans, including those in artistic and cultural endeavors. The authors also offered an encouraging statistic: "The successes of integration and affirmative action created a substantial black middle class: there are now four times as many black families with incomes above $50,000 a year as there were in 1964."[14]

But the economic news is not all positive. Hertzberg and Gates go on to say that the same programs that benefited middle and upper income blacks "have contributed to a distillation of ever more concentrated pools of poverty and despair in the inner cities."[15] Many experts agree, and, based on studies and experience, they argue that the battle against racial discrimination and despair is far from over.

When the magazine *USA Weekend* surveyed almost 250,000 students in grades 6–12 from all over the country, the results were surprising and discouraging. When asked if most people their age carry some form of racial prejudice, 84 percent of the teenagers answered "yes." When asked if they believed that racial tensions will always exist, 86 percent said "yes." As one 15-year-old put it, "I feel accepted by my peers, but some people tell me it's because I 'act white.' What does that mean?"[16] Many black students expressed their belief that things only *seem* to have changed a lot in the last 30 years.

In the workplace, similar anxieties persist. "The majority of the business owners and supervisors are white," one 17-year-old wrote. "It's harder to get a job when you're a young black man."[17] Some statistics strongly support this view. According to the Urban Institute, 53 percent of black men aged 25–34 are either unemployed or earn too little to lift a family of four out of poverty.[18]

The outlook for many women may not be much better. Ann Morrison, author of the book *Breaking the Glass Ceiling,* warns that if the government backs down on affirmative action initiatives, "[companies] are going to shove it on the back burner, because it's difficult and it's draining. The progress that has been made is still so fragile."[19]

An Hispanic female executive checks blueprints. Was she hired because of her gender and ethnic background or because of her talent?

Affirmative action supporters also point out that, if white males really are falling victim to reverse discrimination, why is there still double digit unemployment in the African American community?[20] Why do women continue to be very much in the minority in senior management positions? And why do women who do make it to the top earn salaries that are about one-third lower than male executives who are doing the same job?[21] It may, indeed, be unrealistic to argue that this country is ready and eager for color-blind and gender-blind social policies and that the government should leave hiring decisions up to the goodwill of the institutions involved.

Another argument for affirmative action points to the difference between so-called reverse discrimination and the kind of discrimination that was common in the past, whether based on color, creed, or gender. Traditional discrimination assumed the inferiority of those it excluded. But the kind of "reverse" discrimination that is alleged to occur because of affirmative action does not imply *inferiority*—it carries with it no stigma. The aim of such policies is to *include* rather than to *exclude.*

Furthermore, supporters of affirmative action say that it has become essential to our future. It is projected that by the year 2000, two out of three new workers will be either women or members of minority groups. Many educators say that colleges need to properly prepare their students for future work in a multicultural society. How is such preparation possible without a representative number of minorities and women in the faculty, staff, and student body?[22]

Supporters of affirmative action believe that we—as a society—must make up for inequities of the past. Critics argue that the conditions of the past no longer exist.

Author and editor Nicolaus Mills compiled a wide assortment of views on affirmative action in his 1994 book, *Debating Affirmative Action.* In his introduction to the book, he effectively summarizes both sides of the debate. Speaking for the supporters, he writes, "Affirmative action benefits all. We are better off as a nation when those who run our schools, our businesses, our police departments, reflect our population as a whole. [An] America that ignores the need for such representatives is a nation asking for social turmoil."[23]

OPPOSITION TO AFFIRMATIVE ACTION

Opponents of affirmative action also see social turmoil as an important issue in this debate, but they see the turmoil as a *result* of affirmative action. Nobody denies the impact of past and present discrimination on American life. But critics point out that affirmative action, as it was originally authorized during the 1960s, was inspired by conditions that existed (especially for blacks in the South) at that time—conditions that no longer exist.

The price of affirmative action, opponents argue, is not paid by those who are most guilty of discrimination, and it's not paid by society as a whole, like taxes are paid. Instead, it is innocent third parties, often poor or disadvantaged in their own ways, who pay the price when they lose out on an opportunity due to their race or gender. Mills speaks for many opponents this way:

> The white college student hurt by an affirmative action admissions policy is someone too young to be held responsible for education[al] racism. The blue-collar worker, especially if from a family that

Opponents point out that affirmative action policies sometimes benefit middle-class minority students, who are recruited by colleges as if they were disadvantaged.

immigrated to America in the late nineteenth century, is someone whose ancestors themselves were the victims of discrimination and who has typically not benefited from racism in such a way as to justify losing out on a job simply because of not being a minority.[24]

Another question is raised by critics of affirmative action when they argue that it is almost always *individuals* who discriminate against minorities and women, not whole companies or colleges. Why not simply attack the discriminatory practices of those backward few rather than forcing a great number of unnecessary preferences on the group?

Critics also point out that affirmative action policies have often benefited people who have no right to special consideration, such as a suburban, middle-class, black high school student who is recruited by colleges as if he or she were disadvantaged.

Affirmative action practices, opponents argue, emphasize group rights instead of individual rights and differences among people rather than characteristics they hold in common. Preferential treatment is sanctioned in the name of *diversity,* but critics question how genuine that diversity is when it refers to groups rather than individuals. An artificial diversity can cover up, rather than cure, the disease of continuing inequality. For example, in spite of the appearance of a larger number of black students on college campuses during the early 1990s, only 26 to 28 percent of them graduated from those colleges.[25]

This false sense of diversity on a campus or in a workplace, opponents argue, causes other serious problems. Minorities who appear to be benefiting from affirmative action often end up stigmatized by it. Opponents argue that affirmative action encourages the assumption that minorities wouldn't be at that school or have that job without preferential treatment, and therefore they are seen by others—and sometimes by themselves—as inferior. Many opponents of affirmative action who are themselves part of a minority group are concerned that preferential treatment can promote self-doubt and undermine self-respect. They also worry about how some people who benefit from affirmative action might cling to their status as *victim.* The role of victim guarantees them a certain amount of public sympathy along with opportunities previously denied.[26]

Even those who oppose affirmative action, however, are able to see more and more reason to pursue true diversity. They want schools and workplaces to reflect the differences among American citizens, but they believe affirmative action policies are unnecessary. When business leaders examine the American economy, they recognize that workers and consumers of products are increasingly nonwhite. According to Robert M. Teeter, a Republican pollster who is a member of the board of the United Parcel Service, "Diversity isn't a slogan— it's a reality when you're hiring people everywhere. . . . You could abolish affirmative action tomorrow, and not much would change." The CEOs (chief executive officers) in a poll conducted by *Fortune* magazine agree: 96 percent insist that their companies would not change their affirmative action efforts even if all federal enforcement was abolished.[27]

A UNIQUELY AMERICAN PROBLEM

Why is the issue of affirmative action so difficult to resolve? Is it because people are by nature prejudiced against those who are different from themselves, or because they are motivated mostly by self-interest, or because most people will greedily accept whatever is handed to them? Probably none of the above offers a complete explanation. The debate about affirmative action is not strictly about human nature. It is about the United States as a whole—those values and standards of behavior that make the country uniquely American.

Most Americans believe that equal opportunity must be balanced with hard work and merit.

Some cherished American principles are at work in this conflict: on the one hand, citizens believe that everyone deserves equal opportunities; on the other hand, they hold firmly to the principle that hard work and merit—not involuntary membership in some group —should determine who prospers and who does not.[28]

And that is only one of the contradictions involved. "The real problem," observes Will Marshall, president of the Progressive Policy Institute, "is how to balance two competing, worthwhile values. One is the idea of redressing historical wrongs. The other is the idea that government ought to treat everybody the same. They're both powerful imperatives. Unfortunately, there isn't any neat solution that magically makes the tension between them go away."[29]

It is difficult to overstate the importance of the ongoing battle for and against affirmative action. Manning Marable, author and director of the Institute for Research in African-American Studies at Columbia University, is among those who believe that a "higher ideal" is at stake. It is nothing less than "the ultimate elimination of race and gender inequality, the uprooting of prejudice and discrimination, and the realization of a truly democratic nation."[30]

For a long time after slavery was abolished, "separate but equal" facilities allowed legal forms of racial segregation.

HOW DID WE GET HERE?

"We hold these truths to be self-evident," Thomas Jefferson wrote in the Declaration of Independence, "that all men are created equal, that they are endowed by their Creator with certain unalienable rights, that among these are Life, Liberty, and the pursuit of Happiness." These stirring words do not provoke controversy; they define, in fact, the foundation upon which our freedom as Americans has been built. But such an ideal has not always been easy to put into consistent practice.

During much of American history, it was generally accepted by white people that blacks were not the same kind of human beings as whites and that slavery was the proper role for black people. In the famous 1857 Dred Scott Decision, the Supreme Court declared that no black person—free or slave—could claim U.S. citizenship. It also stated that Congress could not prohibit slavery in U.S. territories.

Even after 1865, when the Civil War ended and slavery was abolished, the government found ways to keep most black Americans securely fixed in a lower status.

In June 1959, Prince Edward County, Virginia, closed all public schools to black children. White children attended private schools—some supported by state funding. Black children attended class in a crowded, one-room shack.

In 1896, for instance, the Supreme Court decision *Plessy v. Ferguson* called for "separate but equal" facilities, and this led to countless forms of segregation actually sanctioned by the government.[1]

The United States made some gradual attempts, however, during the 1950s and 1960s to make up for past wrongs. The 1954 Supreme Court case *Brown v. Board of Education of Topeka, Kansas,* made it illegal to require racial segregation in any school or government-run facility, such as public beaches and city buses. The *Brown* nondiscrimination principle proved to be powerful enough to inspire the most dramatic

civil-rights advance in American history, the passage of
the Civil Rights Act of 1964. Within a few short years—
after passage of the 1965 Voting Rights Act and the
Civil Rights Act of 1968 (also called the Fair Housing
Act)—racial discrimination was at last declared both
wrong and illegal.[2]

Women, also, had been assigned a subservient role
throughout history and were generally considered inferior to men. The suffragist movement (supporters of a
woman's right to vote) successfully won passage of the
Nineteenth Amendment in 1920. The feminist movement that blossomed during the 1960s and 1970s
opened up new opportunities for women by campaign-

**Women worked hard to gain suffrage. Above, they marched
with a banner quoting President Woodrow Wilson's support
of women's right to vote.**

ing for the passage and enforcement of equal rights laws. With widespread activism, public acceptance, and legislation for both women's rights and civil rights, equal opportunity became a universally accepted social goal. However, at this same point in history—during the turbulent 1960s—affirmative action and the battles it inspired actually began.

PRESIDENTS KENNEDY, JOHNSON, AND NIXON

The term *affirmative action* was probably first used and linked to civil rights by President John F. Kennedy shortly after he took office in 1961. By signing Executive Order 10925, he established the president's Equal

Vice President Lyndon Johnson, center, *and Hobart Taylor Jr.,* right, *listened as President John F. Kennedy commended 19 companies that had pledged to cooperate with the Equal Employment Opportunity Commission in 1963.*

In the 1960s, segregation and discrimination against African Americans still existed—especially in the southern states.

Employment Opportunity Commission (EEOC), and he declared that people in the construction industry had certain obligations when doing business with the government. The order stated, "The contractor will take affirmative action to ensure that applicants are employed, and employees are treated during their employment, without regard to their race, creed, color, or national origin."

The language in Kennedy's decree was widely applauded as a bold and important step forward. Boldness was required, because Kennedy specifically intended to warn politicians from Southern states—where segregation was still a fact of life—that job discrimination would not be tolerated in government contracts. His goal of equal opportunity, however, was stated in broad terms. Kennedy's Executive Order said nothing about an actual affirmative action policy aimed at racial balance or representation.[3]

When Kennedy proposed legislation that ultimately became the Civil Rights Act of 1964, he was still aiming primarily at the South. Along with other liberal leaders, Kennedy assumed that if the government banned discrimination, it could create a "level playing field." (This term for equal opportunity was borrowed from baseball, where Jackie Robinson and other black players were able to thrive only after the removal of racial barriers. Robinson was the first black person allowed to play in major league baseball.)[4]

Similar to Executive Order 10925, the language of the Civil Rights Act of 1964 offered no detailed definition of affirmative action. Although Title VII of this bill does prohibit an employer from discriminating because of an "individual's race, color, religion, sex, or national origin," it declares that nothing in the act is designed "to grant preferential treatment to any group because of race, color, religion, sex, or national origin." In fact, the Civil Rights Act of 1964 would never have been passed by Congress if it had attempted to legalize preferences.[5]

Only a year later, however, President Lyndon B. Johnson's administration began to change the language concerning affirmative action. Johnson's key declaration on the topic came in a speech titled "To Fulfill These Rights," delivered at the Howard University commencement in June 1965. After first praising Americans for having knocked down so many racial barriers, Johnson became much more somber in tone. "Freedom is not enough," he declared. "You do not take a person who, for years, has been hobbled by chains and liberate him, bring him to the starting line of a race, and then say, 'You are free to compete with all others and still justly believe you have been completely fair.'"[6]

In 1966 the Department of Labor made the race of employees part of their personnel records. This helped in the evaluation of hiring practices.

This speech made clear Johnson's belief that trying to equalize the "playing field" was not enough. Special help was also needed. Toward this effort, the Department of Labor began to make the race of employees a part of their personnel records in 1966. This information could then be used to evaluate hiring practices. The Labor Department also created the Office of Federal Contract Compliance (OFCC) and began to tighten its affirmative action requirements. Contractors doing government work were required to present a "written affirmative action compliance program" that would "provide in detail for specific steps to guarantee equal employment opportunity keyed to the problems and needs of minority groups, including, when there are deficiencies, the development of specific goals and timetables. . . . "[7]

When President Richard M. Nixon took office in 1969, however, affirmative action was still ill defined and not widely supported. It faced fierce opposition from many congressmen and senators from both parties. Although Nixon's conservative politics were widely known, his administration chose not to alter Johnson's course. In fact, it was under Nixon, not Johnson, that the first official government affirmative action program (the Philadelphia Plan) was pushed through Congress. The unemployment rate of young blacks was high, and Nixon apparently believed that affirmative action could be an important part of the solution to the widespread urban unrest of the late 1960s.

Nixon chose George Shultz to head the Labor Department, and Shultz set the tone clearly and quickly. He made tough demands on the highly segregated con-

George Shultz, secretary of labor under President Richard Nixon in 1969 and 1970, demanded an increase in minority hiring.

struction industry of Philadelphia, requiring more minority hiring and even setting percentages or goals for which contractors should aim. Although such numbers were not rigid at this point, Shultz's action initiated what would ultimately become the most hated aspect of affirmative action—quotas.

In February 1970, the Labor Department issued a new set of affirmative action plans. Order No. 4 was aimed at large government contractors and spoke in terms of requiring proportionate representation of minorities among their employees. The nation, it seemed, had moved even further from the original intent of affirmative action.[8]

THE SUPREME COURT'S ROLE

Citizens soon began bringing affirmative action cases to court—sometimes all the way to the Supreme Court. Many people wondered whether the new affirmative action policies could hold up under this kind of legal scrutiny. Surprisingly, they did.

In March 1971, one case—*Griggs v. Duke Power Company*—shaped affirmative action thinking for the next two decades. The black petitioners claimed that in order to get hired by Duke Power they needed a high school diploma or they had to pass an intelligence test. They argued that this violated their rights under Title VII. In an 8-to-0 decision, the Supreme Court ruled in favor of the petitioners. Duke Power's requirements, the justices said, acted as "built-in headwinds" against minorities, and that was enough to make the requirements illegal.[9]

That case opened the way for affirmative action to expand still further. In December 1971, the Labor Department made permanent a Revised Order No. 4 that specifically included women in the "affected class" it was designed to protect. Universities also began to come under affirmative action scrutiny during the Nixon years. Columbia University, for example, had to submit three different affirmative action plans before finally getting back the $13 million in federal funding that had been taken away because of the school's hiring policies regarding women and minorities.[10]

Affirmative action continued to expand under Democratic president Jimmy Carter. By the end of the 1970s, views of affirmative action were developing in dramatic ways in both the federal government and the

Supreme Court. Between 1978 and 1980 the Court rendered three decisions—one in education and two in employment—that changed the judicial and political climate surrounding affirmative action.

Perhaps the most famous of such Supreme Court cases occurred in 1978—*Regents of the University of California v. Allan Bakke* (usually referred to simply as *Bakke*). Allan Bakke, a white medical school applicant, charged that he had been discriminated against by the University of California's admission program. Several students had been admitted under a special program for members of minority groups. Bakke had been

Minorities throughout the country protested the reverse discrimination claim of Allan Bakke, a white male.

The Supreme Court ruled in favor of Allan Bakke (second from left) *and against the University of California's special admissions policy.*

rejected even though his test scores were higher than those of the minority students who had been admitted. Bakke claimed that his application had been rejected only because he was white.

The Supreme Court issued a two-part decision (5–4) in favor of Bakke. In the first part, five justices ruled against the school's special admissions program and ordered Bakke admitted. Four justices based their decision on the Civil Rights Act of 1964, which prohibits discrimination by a school receiving federal funds. The fifth justice, Lewis F. Powell Jr., based his decision on the Fourteenth Amendment to the Constitution, which guarantees all citizens equal protection under the law.

Powell issued an additional opinion, which formed the second part of the Court's decision. He stated that schools could consider race or ethnic background as one factor among others in determining admissions. Powell's opinion was supported by the four remaining justices, who had upheld the school's plan. The decision was widely regarded as a compromise that did not help schools determine how to achieve a desired racial mix of students without imposing racial quotas. The Supreme Court decisions that followed, however, were not so tentative and created a strong legal precedent for upholding preferential treatment.

COUNTERREVOLUTION

By the time the Carter administration came to an end, the American public was becoming disenchanted with the whole issue of affirmative action. The Court had tried, it seemed, to make a distinction between a goal and a quota, between a voluntary plan and a required plan, and between what the Civil Rights Act of 1964 allowed and what it prohibited. But to most citizens at the time, it seemed like baffling legal double-talk.

The stage was set for the counterrevolution of the 1980s, especially when a conservative Republican, Ronald Reagan, became president of the United States in 1981. As a candidate, Reagan had promised to end affirmative action if he was elected. "We must not allow," Reagan declared, "the noble concept of equal opportunity to be distorted into federal guidelines or quotas which require race, ethnicity, or sex—rather than ability and qualifications—to be the principal factor in hiring or education."[11]

As president, Ronald Reagan appointed justices Sandra Day O'Connor (standing second from right), *Antonin Scalia* (standing at far left), *and Anthony M. Kennedy (standing at far right), all of whom opposed affirmative action.*

As president, Reagan appointed Supreme Court justices who opposed affirmative action. He also severely cut the budgets of the Equal Employment Opportunity Commission and the Office of Federal Contract Compliance, crippling the ability of both agencies to pursue affirmative action cases. Many experts claim that the Reagan administration, in effect, killed the federal policy of affirmative action.[12]

By the time President George Bush took office in 1989, civil rights groups had rallied and regained some of their earlier power. They began to pressure the administration and Congress for additional legislation. The Civil Rights Act of 1990 (which was passed a year later—after formidable opposition—as the Civil Rights Act of 1991) was written in reaction to several Supreme Court decisions. The Court had been showing more and more leniency toward employers. Minorities and women who would easily have won their discrimination cases prior to 1989 found themselves on the losing side. The Civil Rights Act of 1990 had attempted to strengthen protections against employment discrimination for racial minorities and women.

President Bill Clinton's initial cabinet (center forefront) *contained three women, four African Americans, and two Hispanics. He wanted his entire staff to "look like America."*

Despite accusations of sexual harassment by attorney Anita Hill (below), *the appointment of Clarence Thomas* (above) *to the Supreme Court was confirmed by the U.S. Senate.*

Bush initially fought many aspects of the bill because he felt it established employment quotas. But ultimately he had no choice but to sign the Civil Rights Act of 1991. The country was in turmoil over racial and gender issues, especially after Bush's appointee to the Supreme Court—Clarence Thomas—was accused of sexual harassment by attorney Anita Hill. Although Thomas prevailed and took his seat on the Court, the televised and highly controversial Senate hearings changed the political and social atmosphere of the nation for years to come. After the Thomas appointment, Bush thought he needed to prove to the American public that he was not racist or sexist, so he signed the Civil Rights Act of 1991.[13]

Then, in the final debate of the 1992 campaign, Democratic presidential candidate Bill Clinton said, "I don't think we've got a person to waste. I owe the American people a White House staff, a cabinet, and appointments that look like America but that meet high standards of excellence, and that's what I'll do."[14]

When he was elected president, Clinton made sure that his initial cabinet—with three women, four African Americans, and two Hispanics—was diverse. The new president was signaling the country that on matters of race and gender he was going to be different from his predecessors. But affirmative action continued to be a backlash issue to those excluded from its benefits, and it fueled a politics of resentment.[15]

WHERE ARE WE NOW?

What is perhaps most disturbing about this issue is that, three decades after the first affirmative action programs were established, Americans can't agree about why or if we need them. Compared to earlier civil rights legislation, affirmative action has produced no sense of optimism. Nor has it earned a consensus about the future.

Author Nicolaus Mills sums up the stark contrast between current and past discussion about race in this way:

> In the South of the 1960s, eliminating a whites-only drinking fountain or desegregating a dual school system provided a clear remedy for a wrong. Such action produced visible results and brought immediate relief to the victims or the children of the victims of discrimination. But increasingly, affirmative action cases have resisted neat cause-and-effect solutions or a sense of being confined to a limited period of time. The result in the 1990s is an affirmative action debate in which all sides can point to the burdens imposed on them and simultaneously claim the moral high ground.[16]

Furthermore, those opposed to affirmative action say that the initial intent and goal of nondiscrimination was sabotaged by court interpretations and administrative policies that did the exact opposite. Steven Yates is one of the most outspoken of those opponents, and in his book *Civil Wrongs* he says, "Instead of being replaced by genuinely color-blind and gender-blind practices, legally sanctioned discrimination against blacks, other minorities, and women came to be replaced by legally sanctioned discrimination against white men."[17]

Others disagree. They point to hard evidence that discrimination against minorities and women is still very real and complaints about reverse discrimination are dangerous attempts to undo the progress that has been made.

Perhaps the biggest source of conflict in this debate is that certain core questions remain unanswered. For example, what kinds of discrimination exist in this country and what remedies are needed to aid its victims? Will there ever be a point at which we can actually say that affirmative action remedies have served their purpose and should therefore be put to an end?[18]

Students at the University of Michigan demonstrate in favor of the school's affirmative action policy.

RACIAL
DISCRIMINATION

Is the United States a nation of racists? As we approach the twenty-first century, what has changed—and what has failed to change—about the way Americans hate, mistrust, fear, attack, and stereotype each other based solely on the color of their skin?

There is probably more heated disagreement about racism than any other aspect of affirmative action. If racism is still a cultural reality, then perhaps we still need affirmative action policies, but if it no longer exists except in the history books, then affirmative action has outlived its purpose.

Most Americans would probably say that we've made enormous progress since the days of lynchings and "whites only" drinking fountains, but they would also admit that racist attitudes and behavior still exist. The viewpoints of many other people, however, are more extreme. One side says that Americans are more racist than ever, but they are more subtle about it. The other side says *enough* to all the finger-pointing,

47

Although the African American man and the white man are both managers, they may experience life in the United States quite differently.

blaming, and cries of racism because it's essentially a dead issue.

VIEWPOINT: RACISM IS EVERYWHERE

Television viewers in 1991 could watch a fifteen-minute segment of the ABC program *PrimeTime Live* showing that it may still be a distinct disadvantage to have black skin. For this broadcast from St. Louis, Missouri, reporters and hidden cameras followed two young men of equal education, sophistication and affluence. The only difference between the two was that one was black and the other white.

The men were videotaped in a variety of encounters with shoe salesmen, record-store employees, rental agents, landlords, employment agencies, taxicab drivers, and ordinary citizens. With astonishing consistency, the black man was either ignored or given special and suspicious attention. Store clerks asked him to pay higher prices for the same products; car dealers asked him for larger down payments for the same car; landlords turned him away as a prospective tenant; cab drivers refused to pick him up.[1]

After watching this broadcast, it is easy to speculate that even though the two young men appeared to be so much alike, their lives would be quite different. The black man would be more likely than his white counterpart to experience daily encounters that would chip away at his self-esteem and self-confidence. And he would certainly be more likely to go through life angry and with a growing sense of injustice.

Was this an isolated incident? A case of slanted journalism? Many people say *no*—the show reflected the reality of racism.

The situation is not much different for other minorities even when they, in fact, make up the *majority* of the population of an area. Author Ruben Navarrette Jr., for example, points out that although his home town in California is over 72 percent Mexican American, racial stereotypes still dictate how the city functions. Only certain types of jobs are believed to be appropriate for the Mexican-American citizens, and none of these are positions of power. The fire chief, police chief, mayor, and all other major city government leaders are white. Only 10 of the 200 teachers in the school system are Mexican American, and there has never been a Latino principal or superintendent of schools.[2]

Many experts on issues of race and justice point to the 1995 trial of O. J. Simpson as a defining moment

Double murder defendant O. J. Simpson (left) *listens to the not-guilty verdict with his attorneys. Reaction to the Simpson verdict differed dramatically between blacks and whites, as can be seen among these college students in Rock Island, Illinois* (right).

for race relations in the United States. For 16 months— from the night that Simpson's ex-wife and a friend were brutally murdered until the jury reached its verdict of not guilty—millions of Americans had eagerly consumed every detail of the case presented to them by the media. When the verdict was read, approximately 150 million Americans stopped what they were doing in their homes and workplaces to watch the live television coverage. The evidence against Simpson had seemed to be overwhelming to many people, but the jury—mostly black individuals—took only a few hours to find "reasonable doubt" of his guilt and, therefore, declare him not guilty.

A huge portion of black America celebrated the verdict. The trial had seemed to support a common belief among blacks that law enforcement officers were blatantly racist and couldn't be trusted. Finally justice had prevailed for a black man unjustly accused by white society. One network showed black law students at Howard University in Washington, D.C., screaming and jumping for joy. The streets of many black neighborhoods became filled with people cheering the news and honking their car horns in approval.

Meanwhile, much of white America expressed disbelief and outrage that justice had been mocked, that a wife beater and alleged murderer had been set free. Cheering seemed outrageous to those who focused on the two dead, mutilated victims and their grieving families. As a jubilant party took place in Simpson's house, protesters gathered outside to chant, "murderer, murderer." Many white observers of the trial saw what they believed to be shocking proof that blacks were worse racists than whites because they placed more importance on racial solidarity than on justice.

Suddenly, the divide between blacks and whites seemed to widen dramatically, and many people of all races felt a profound sense of despair. For example, the Reverend Eugene Rivers, the leader of a black church congregation in inner-city Boston, said, "This is accelerating America's descent into a state of psychological apartheid. The level of polarization is amazing."[3]

Civil rights activist and leader Myrlie Evers-Williams relates how a white man accidentally bumped into her in a hotel lobby, called her a "black bitch," and then stomped off.[4] Although she says hostile treatment is "nothing new" to her and many African Americans, this particularly shocking incident occurred on the day of the Simpson verdict when such examples of racial hostility seemed to be everywhere. Evers-Williams was married to Medgar Evers, a civil rights worker who was murdered in Mississippi on June 12, 1963. She said that the aftermath of the Simpson trial provided "clear documentation that we are a divided society. Those who thought we were doing extremely well . . . are wrong."[5]

The Simpson case was not the only one that created tension, however. With all the media coverage of violence and crime among blacks, many whites have developed an unreasonable and destructive fear of all blacks—especially young males. Although fear of being victimized is inevitable in this violence-saturated culture, imagine how this subtle form of racism feels from the point of view of the majority of black males.

When 31-year-old Robert Mackey got into an elevator in an Atlanta, Georgia, office building with two other black men, the white female on the elevator jumped out just as the door was about to close. The black men were stunned. "We were three well-dressed, well-groomed men going to work," says Mackey, "and it is outrageous that this woman would act as if she was unsafe in [our] presence."[6]

That woman would probably deny being racist, and she may have regretted offending the men. Her actions would be defended by some as merely a form of self-defense, based on her perception of the danger black males represent to her as a white female. Only the most extreme racists cling to the notion that the African American race is inferior, but targeting the behavior of individuals is another matter, especially the behavior of poor, inner city blacks.[7]

Roger Wilkins, a history professor at George Mason University in Fairfax, Virginia, says that "blacks and whites experience America very differently," and he strongly disagrees with those who say that racism is a thing of the past.[8] He said:

> I know of *no* blacks, rich or poor, who haven't been hurt in some measure by the racism in this country. The current mood . . . completely ignores the fact that some blacks never escaped the straight line of oppression that ran from slavery through the semislavery of sharecropping to the late mid-century migration from Southern farms into isolated pockets of urban poverty. Their families have always been excluded, . . . and so they were utterly defenseless when the enormous American economic dislocations that began in the mid-1970s slammed into their communities, followed closely by deadly waves of crack cocaine.[9]

Wilkins claims that whites appear to feel that they own America—a land of opportunity that is superior to any other country in the world—and that they are entitled to whatever good things it offers. Some whites, according to Wilkins, feel that "the presence of blacks messes everything up."[10]

No other minority group experiences as much isolation as blacks, according to sociologists Douglas Massey and Nancy Denton.

Not all acts of discrimination are direct and overt. When Wilkens was speaking to a group of college students, one of them said that whites give him looks that seem to ask, "What are *you* doing here?" Wilkins asked when that occurred, and the student replied, "Every time I walk in a door." At that moment, Wilkins said every black person in the room nodded with recognition.[11]

In their 1993 book *American Apartheid,* sociologists Douglas Massey and Nancy Denton put the blame for race relations on the *degree* of segregation that still exists in America. No other group, including Hispanics, experiences as much isolation as blacks. The authors point out that over one-third of America's blacks live in 16 metropolitan areas, packed "tightly around the urban core. In plain terms, they live in ghettos."[12]

The New Yorker's special report on race describes a shocking degree of suffering: "Half of all African American children live in poverty. A third of all black men between the ages of 20 and 29 are entangled in the criminal-justice system. The leading cause of death among young black men is gunshot wounds."[13]

Under conditions such as these, it should not be surprising when African Americans have a different view about racism than whites. A 1995 *Washington Post* survey found that 68 percent of blacks (and only 38 percent of whites) believe racism is still a major problem in America.

This child lives only five blocks from the U.S. Capitol, but his home is in a ghetto—one of Washington, D. C.'s poorer black neighborhoods.

Teenagers appear to have a special perspective because they are at an age characterized by a powerful need to "belong," and race provides the most obvious visual identity. Add to this the problem of peer pressure and the fact that teens often have to seek out the safety and security of same-race groups, and the potential for racial confrontation is an everyday threat. A 1993 Louis Harris poll of high school students found that 75 percent had witnessed confrontations motivated by race or religion.[14]

In a national survey distributed by *USA Weekend* in 1994, thousands of young people had plenty to say about the topic of race:

> On the first day of my new school, some classmates wondered why I was in honors classes. Their questions were answered when I received high A's on my first tests. Still, it seems some teachers don't expect as much of me. Sometimes the teacher comes by and I don't have my homework done, but she keeps going. For other students, she'll stop and ask. I think she assumes it's normal for me not to do as well. I'm a minority student—what more can you expect?
> —Erica Waples, age 15, Lewes, Delaware

> Someday all people will be equal. But I don't think I'll see that day. I'm half East Indian and half Filipino. And because of that, kids have picked on me, called me names and even made fun of the things my mom makes me for lunch.
> —Ravi Jain, age 12, Rochester Hills, Michigan

> Once I got into a fight with three black kids. I called them names, like "nigger"—a word I had learned only two weeks before and didn't really

Teenagers often feel a special need to "belong." Race provides a strong visual sense of identity.

understand. I was just a kid. Later, about six black guys came up to me. They didn't yell; they just told me they should kick my butt and then told me to apologize. I did. After that, everything got better.

—Dallas Johnson, age 15, Fond du Lac, Wisconsin

Last year I was browsing in a store. The clerk kept staring at me. Then she pointed to a sign: "Shoplifters will be prosecuted." I didn't know what was happening. I felt scared. Then I figured it out. . . . The lady was white, and I am Salvadoran, so she must have thought I was going to steal something.

—Wendy Hernandez, age 13, Brooklyn, New York

I used to not be prejudiced at all. In fact, I used to walk around downtown Detroit by myself. My parents told me I had to be more careful. But I thought they were just being mean. Prejudiced.

> Since I was beaten up [by three black female members of a gang], my views have changed. . . . My black friends feel bad for me, but they're afraid of these girls, too. Now when I'm out in public I find myself singling out people of color. I feel guilty about it, but how would you feel if those girls had attacked you?
> —Maureen McInerney, age 16, Plymouth, Michigan [15]

Not all of the information gained by the editors of *USA Weekend* was negative, however. Despite the teenagers' stories and concerns about racism, the survey did show that teens of different races are getting together and reaching out to each other, at least on a one-to-one basis. Most of the respondents (72 percent)

Despite concerns about racism, teens of different races are reaching out to each other, at least on a one-to-one basis.

reported having a close friend of another race. More than seven out of ten said they would date someone of another race. More than half declared racial diversity in their schools to be a "good thing." And more than half expect that they will live to see the election of a president who is a minority.[16]

What about affirmative action? These teenagers' views were not drawn along color lines. The results show that 90 percent of all who took the survey say race should not be a factor in employment opportunities and college admissions.[17]

Many people agree, and one of the most powerful arguments against affirmative action is that it actually *causes* a "new racism" that has grown out of preferential treatment for blacks. This new racism, according to author Charles Murray, is seen to be most apparent and damaging among whites who are the most educated, affluent, and powerful people in the country. Even though the new racists do not think blacks are inferior and may even have been active supporters of civil rights, they do think about and treat blacks differently based solely on their race. The results can be just as bad as any created by the "old racism."[18]

During the last few decades, many businesses and schools found themselves accused of violating Title VII of the Civil Rights Act of 1964, and the best way to combat such an accusation was to interview, hire, and admit enough minority candidates to be in compliance with the law. It became common practice in the selection process to provide an edge if the minorities who were available weren't also the best qualified candidates. Such an edge may have taken the form of lower-

To combat accusations of discrimination, many companies used a different set of standards to hire members of minority groups.

ing the required test scores for minorities or even providing different tests.[19]

This kind of preferential treatment has often led to resentment and condescension. And it perpetuates myths about racial inferiority. "The system," writes Murray, "segments whites and blacks who come in contact with each other so as to maximize the likelihood that whites have the advantage in experience and ability. The system then encourages both whites and blacks to behave in ways that create self-fulfilling prophecies even when no real differences exist."[20] The new racism and the old racism are not unrelated. Preferential treatment for minorities provides persuasive evidence for the old racists who are saying, "We told you so."

VIEWPOINT: RACISM IS OVER

Charles Murray is among those who believe that, although racism in all its forms may not be entirely dead, "there is an abiding desire [in American institutions today] to be non-racist. This need can be construed as brotherly love. Guilt will do as well. But the civil rights movement did its job." Murray also says that preferential treatment is "not holding many doors open to qualified blacks that would otherwise be closed." [21]

Author Dinesh D'Souza, one of the most controversial figures in this debate, wrote his first book, *Illiberal*

Author Dinesh D'Souza opposes affirmative action.

Education, as an attack on affirmative action, political correctness, and multiculturalism on college campuses. D'Souza argues that policies that discriminate *for* any one group are as wrong as policies that discriminate *against* it.[22]

In D'Souza's second, even more controversial book, *The End of Racism,* he claims that white racism has all but disappeared. D'Souza claims that racism did not develop out of evil or ignorance, but out of rational and scientific attempts to explain and simplify this diverse world. Whatever racial discrimination still exists he sees as "rational discrimination." For example, since so many violent criminals are young black males, taxi drivers, store owners, and employers are being rational (not racist) when they ignore, refuse to conduct business with, or refuse to hire black males.[23]

Many people adamantly disagree with D'Souza's views, however. A book review in *Newsweek,* for example, accused D'Souza of "offering solace to those whites who wish to wash their hands of responsibility for black problems."[24] And an outraged William Raspberry, in his column for the *Washington Post,* summed up what he considered D'Souza's distorted view of the past as follows: "Slavery wasn't all that bad a deal for black folk, and besides, there was nothing racial about it. Segregation was created by the Southern ruling class 'to *protect* blacks.' Only 'an infinitesimal fraction of the black population' was lynched."[25]

More mainstream are the views of Joseph G. Conti and Brad Stetson, who provided a thoughtful insiders' view of racism in their Special Report for the January 1996 issue of *Destiny* Magazine. "Many liberals, black and white," according to these authors, "have been essentially programmed to see racism where it doesn't exist, and to attribute to racism virtually any hardship or difficulty minorities encounter. Yet, there has never been a time in the history of this country when racism was as powerless as it is today."[26]

Conti and Stetson contend that antiblack racism is committed by individuals, not institutions. They assert that there is "no large scale conspiracy to impede the progress of blacks."[27] Seeing racism everywhere, according to Conti and Stetson, convinces too many black Americans that their situation is hopeless and causes too many to give up before they even try to succeed. What the authors call "racial hype" promotes the idea that the system is rigged and that "whitey" is waiting in ambush. If young African Americans believe their dreams will be destroyed because of racism, they will ultimately stop dreaming altogether.

Conti and Stetson list several encouraging statistics, including the following:

- Blacks earning $50,000 a year or more are the fastest growing income group in America.
- Since the 1960s, the percentage of affluent black Americans has more than doubled.
- In families where both parents are college educated and both parents work, black families make more than white families. This is the case in all parts of the United States, for families of all ages.
- Between 1979 and 1991, the number of black accountants increased by 479 percent, the number of black lawyers by 280 percent, and the number of black computer programmers by 343 percent.[28]

Since the 1960s, the percentage of affluent black Americans has more than doubled. Is this encouraging statistic the result of affirmative action policies?

While many people argue that such progress indicates that affirmative action is no longer needed, others point out that these dramatic advances would have been impossible without affirmative action policies and that many goals for minorities remain elusive. Still, isn't it possible to attain these goals without further government intervention? One of the quiet triumphs of affirmative action has been what newspaper columnist Tom Teepen calls "the revolution it has wrought in black expectations. Ambition finally makes sense."[29] Although this may seem a fragile revolution to some, including Teepen, others see a strong foundation on which to build black self-respect and a new, much-needed sense of responsibility.

Jesse Peterson is the director of BOND, a nationwide organization dedicated to helping young black males grow into responsible manhood. Peterson argues that "so-called black leaders—the traitors of the civil rights movement—have brainwashed black people into obsessively thinking about, and focusing on, racism. It is very unhealthy. It's really a kind of mental slavery, which is even worse than physical slavery. At least in physical slavery your mind and spirit are free, but in mental slavery—which is sadly the state of much of black America today—the deepest part of a person is bound. For black Americans today, this mental bondage has caused anger, withdrawal from the economic mainstream, and an absence of free thought."[30]

According to Conti and Stetson, "The real barriers to black progress in this country are inside the black community itself." As evidence of this, they offer the following national trends among African American communities:
- black out-of-wedlock birthrate (nearly 70 percent)
- violent crime (40 percent of all murder victims are black men killed by other black men)
- black "leadership" (which constantly refuses to face these facts and openly address them, instead habitually pointing to the convenient ghost of racism, and saying over and over, "It's his fault!")[31]

Likewise, most of the remedies for such unfortunate trends lie within the black community itself, according to Conti and Stetson.

Latino stores thrive in the Washington Heights section of New York City.

Many Americans seem to believe that the only major racial conflict in America is between blacks and whites. In a 1996 interview for *Harpers,* author and Berkeley professor Jorge Klor de Alva points out how strange it is that the media has ignored the tension between the country's largest historical minority—blacks—and its largest future one—Latinos. According to federal government estimates, Latinos (referred to as Hispanics by the U.S. Census Bureau) will outnumber blacks in 15 years, as they already do in 21 states.[32]

The complex problems discussed throughout this book apply to Latinos and other minorities as well as blacks. Consider the following percentages of American families below the poverty line: Hispanic 26.2%, black 31.3 %, white 9.4%.[33]

Why are Latinos usually ignored in the racial debate? According to Klor de Alva, ". . . blacks are the central metaphor for otherness and oppression in the U.S."[34] He also says, "Every time we've seen huge numbers of immigrants enter the U.S., the people most devastated by their arrival, in terms of being relegated to an even lower rung on the employment ladder, have been blacks."[35]

THE QUEST FOR DIVERSITY

Affirmative action policies are intended not only to provide equal opportunities for all people; they are also meant to help schools and workplaces achieve an atmosphere of diversity. It was generally thought that greater diversity would mean more racial harmony, but many observers say the opposite has occurred. Author and *New York Daily News* columnist Jim Sleeper is among those who claim that when colleges all over the country began to feel the overwhelming pressure to achieve diversity, many of them responded by accepting a disproportionate number of black students who were unable to meet the school's usual high admission standards.

What was the result? Sleeper says that so many of these students struggled to keep up that even their better-qualified black classmates began to suffer from white resentment and stereotyping. In response, many black students became defensive and withdrawn, and racial tension began to build on these campuses.[36]

Consider these examples:

- In 1988, a poster tacked up in one University of Michigan classroom read: "Support the KKK college fund. A mind is a terrible thing to waste, especially on a 'nigger.'"
- In April 1989 at prestigious Smith College, four black women received anonymous notes containing racial epithets. These incidents led to protests and rallies that included shouting matches between black and white students.
- In 1991, sorority women at the University of Alabama attended a "Who Rides the Bus" party in

When colleges accepted a large number of black students who did not meet the usual admission standards, even the better-qualified black students suffered resentment from white students.

blackface and dressed as poor, pregnant black women. Black students and faculty members marched in protest.[37]

Minority students and supporters have grown increasingly militant in response to such incidents. And the most typical response from school administrations is to push even more strongly for diversity. Ironically, however, the logic that makes people push for more affirmative action programs in order to achieve the ideal of diversity actually tends to *suppress* diverse viewpoints. Dissent is often denounced as "politically incorrect" or even "racist." According to Sleeper, "The pursuit of diversity becomes more divisive than whatever racism the students may have brought with them to college."[38]

For many years, barriers prevented women from getting jobs in the construction industry. Such jobs previously seemed to require a man's physical strength.

GENDER DISCRIMINATION

I think people gravitate toward people who are like them—who talk like them, act like them, look like them. And that means without affirmative action programs, a lot of white males won't let people like me in. The attitude is, "It's our playground, and we decide who comes into it."
—Vela McClam Mitchell[1]

I think affirmative action has done a lot. However, past a certain point, you can't mandate that sort of thing. If other people see you as a woman as having gotten a position just because she is female, you're going to have a lot of people out to show she's incompetent. But if affirmative action programs were taken away tomorrow, I'm not really sure how big an impact it would have. I don't see women getting fired across the board. I don't see that women all of a sudden will stop advancing.
—Marion Dobson DeForest [2]

Affirmative action has come under attack from several fronts, but it is usually debated as a racial issue. Women, however, are not afraid of saying, "Wait a minute—what about us?"

National surveys express strong opposition to affirmative action programs for minorities. But polls conducted during the mid-1990s by the Gallup Organization and the *New York Times* found that the public favors—by as much as 50 percent to 40 percent—preferential treatment for women in hiring for jobs and admission to schools.[3]

Feminist group leaders are not surprised that the debate over affirmative action has focused primarily on race and has avoided the gender issue. According to Leslie Wolfe, president of the Center for Women's Policy Studies, "In a very cynical way, the assault on affirmative action has been framed as a racial issue to persuade white women that they need to choose race over sex. It's a wicked approach. It's an attempt to divide and conquer."[4]

Diverting the terms of the debate away from race is not an easy task. Political analysts argue that women may never build a political movement to counter the deep resentment over racial preference. Even Patricia Ireland, president of the National Organization for Women, acknowledges that women, no less than anyone else, "want to see themselves as personally meritorious and having moved forward because of their own merit—not because of affirmative action."[5]

But many feminist groups have, in fact, rallied in defense of affirmative action. The main point they try to convey is that *it has worked.* Judith Lichtman, president of the Women's Legal Defense Fund, says that what will make the difference in the debate is "Women of every color and nationality, including white women, knowing and understanding that affirmative action has

Patricia Ireland, president of the National Organization for Women, argues that women want to see themselves moving forward because of personal merit, not because of affirmative action.

made a difference for them and not being willing to sign on to rhetoric that is not in their interest or their family's interest."[6]

According to the U.S. Bureau of Labor Statistics, the percentage of women holding executive, administrative, and managerial jobs increased from 32.4 percent to 42 percent during the decade between 1983 and 1993.[7] A 1995 study by Rutgers University Law School professor Alfred Blumrosen (a Labor Department consultant on affirmative action issues) shows that approximately six million women wouldn't have the jobs they have were it not for the inroads made by affirmative action.[8]

In spite of the progress American women have made in the last few decades, many feminists point to evidence that the so-called level playing field is still an illusion. They claim that growing up female in this country often means being overlooked and undervalued by teachers and sexually harassed by male peers. Furthermore, this treatment starts as early as elementary school.

Discrimination based on gender is deeply rooted in American tradition. Throughout history, women have been discouraged or even barred from what the culture determined to be "men's work." They were told that women didn't have the intellectual, mental, or physical attributes to compete with men as equals. A woman's proper place was at home, bearing and raising children. But thanks in part to two world wars, women began to enter the workforce in ever increasing numbers, first because they had no choice, but eventually because many *wanted* to work outside the home.

Early in the twentieth century, the status of women in the workplace took a turn that seemed to make good sense at the time, but for which women are still paying a price. At that time, working conditions in many factories and stores were extremely unpleasant and even dangerous. Social reformers and trade union members fought for labor legislation that would "protect" women by providing shorter hours, plenty of rest periods, and proper sanitation and ventilation. Although

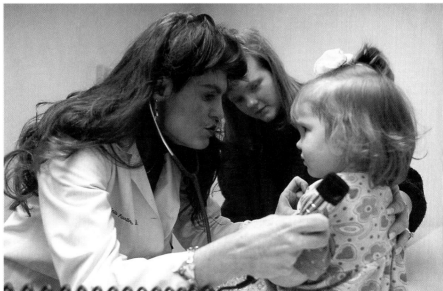

A black female lawyer consults with a client (top), *and a female doctor treats a young patient* (bottom).

During World War II, women, such as this steel cutter, held jobs traditionally held by men.

this kind of special legislation for female workers seemed like the best way to protect their health and ability to be effective mothers, these remedies also put women into a legally protected group. It soon became clear that, as members of a "class" of workers, women were giving up their right to be treated as individuals in the workforce.[9]

During the 1940s and 1950s, working conditions improved for almost *all* workers, but remnants of the notion of a "protected class" still remained. This notion opened a debate about whether "protection" wasn't simply being used as an excuse to discriminate against women who wished to compete fairly with men for jobs.

Diane Joyce won a landmark Supreme Court ruling to help get women into higher-ranking jobs.

Then along came Title VII of the Civil Rights Act, which prohibited discrimination in the labor force. Title VII also began eliminating the special-treatment legislation that had been enacted earlier. For the first time, women were able to appeal for federal legislative protection against intentional discrimination by their employers.[10]

However, most of the wording and intent of the early civil rights legislation reflected concern only for race and ethnicity. For women, the law was not very well developed or interpreted. It was rarely enforced until the Supreme Court heard a landmark case in 1987. The Court made history on March 25, 1987, when it ruled that in order to correct "a manifest imbalance in traditionally segregated job categories," a woman was entitled to a job dispatching road crews in California. With this decision, the Court made clear that affirmative action plans should take into account the sex of underrepresented workers as well as their race.[11]

This controversial case occurred because a 42-year-old widow named Diane Joyce had benefited from the voluntary affirmative action policy of Santa Clara County, California. She had received a job promotion for which she was as qualified as her closest male competitor (although she *was* ranked slightly lower by a subjective, all-male board). When Paul, the man who lost the job to Joyce, sued, the Supreme Court upheld the county's decision to hire the first female road-maintenance worker (among 238 males). The decision cleared up much of the fuzziness in affirmative action plans and ultimately gave Joyce a slight edge for the job in a male-dominated field.

Not surprisingly, however, many people were angry. They pointed to this case as one of the definitive examples of reverse discrimination, and—tending to ignore Joyce's undisputed qualifications for the job—accused the court of choosing gender over merit. As columnist Ellen Goodman wrote at the time of the decision, what she heard was "the low and lingering rumble of those who believe that affirmative action is a pole used by inferior candidates to jump over their superiors."[12]

Goodman argued that the Court made clear it was supporting a fair affirmative action plan because it "didn't discharge a white male, it didn't set up quotas, and, most of all, it didn't give preference to women whose only credentials were in their chromosomes. It

In Detroit, Michigan, members of the Service Employees Union support the continuation of affirmative action policies.

said, in essence, that a subjective two-point difference between Diane and Paul wasn't as important as a 238-job difference between men and women."[13]

The barriers that still remain for women are not only in the kinds of jobs that previously appeared to require a man's physical strength, as in the case of Diane Joyce. Despite the past three decades of affirmative action, "glass ceilings" and "concrete walls" still block many women from top management jobs. According to a federal commission's 1995 report, "White men, while constituting about 43 percent of the workforce, hold about 95 percent of senior management positions, defined as vice president and above. . . . "[14]

As secretary of labor, Robert Reich chaired a bipartisan commission that studied the effects of affirmative action.

This 20-member commission included 10 Republicans and 10 Democrats in the fields of law and labor. Its chairman, former secretary of labor Robert Reich, hailed the report as "a step toward bipartisanship." The commission's report appeared, however, just in time to have an impact on the 1996 elections. Affirmative action emerged as one of the most important "wedge" issues—an issue on which the two parties are separated by their opposing views. The report concluded (through interviews with chief executives) that "Corporate leaders are talking the talk of inclusion. Yet minorities and women express dismay and anger when they describe what they perceive to be innumerable obstacles to their corporate advancement. In short, there is a difference between what corporate leadership says it wants to happen and what is actually happening."[15]

Reich further summed up the findings of the commission by saying, "Affirmative action in all respects is about plans and goals, not quotas and preferences. It's one thing when white men talk about minorities and feel affirmative action is unfair. It's another thing when white men see the difficulties their wives and daughters have moving up the ranks."[16]

Many white students felt bitter about UCLA's preferential treatment of minorities in its admissions policy. In 1997, the policy changed so that race, ethnicity, and gender could no longer be used as factors in the admissions process.

CALIFORNIA AS
A CASE STUDY

"It's unfortunate that they don't want us here anymore and that we've got to fight our way back into this university," said Shauna Robinson, a senior at the University of California, Los Angeles and head of UCLA's African Student Union. "I don't think they ever wanted us here."

But Stacy Gallandt, a senior at Venice High School in Los Angeles, expressed a different view. Stacy, who is white, was turned down by the university's San Diego campus despite her A average, while a Hispanic friend with slightly lower grades was accepted. "They say they haven't got enough room, and that's where other factors come in, like, if you're a minority." [1]

What prompts this kind of debate—which often turns bitter and angry? It's not only that California's university system is highly valued for both its academic reputation and its appealing campus atmosphere. Nor is the problem simply one of too many applicants. (UCLA had 28,000 applicants for its 3,650 freshman slots in the fall of 1996.) The problem, according to many California citizens and policy makers, is one of fairness. UCLA is one of many schools that routinely favored black and Hispanic applicants over whites and Asian Americans (with better credentials) in the name of affirmative action. But that situation has changed.[2]

As of the fall of 1997, the University of California Board of Regents no longer allowed its nine campuses to use race, ethnicity, or gender as primary factors in their admissions process. The number of Hispanic and black students at UCLA is expected to decline by 40 or 50 percent.[3]

By the mid-1990s, universities and colleges found themselves on the front line of the affirmative action battle. Admissions and scholarship practices were put under increased scrutiny by a number of important court rulings and administrative decisions. In March 1996, for example, the Fifth U.S. Circuit Court of Appeals ruled that public universities could not use different admission standards for minority students than they did for white applicants. The court's decision in favor of four white students who were rejected by the University of Texas law school challenged the law of the land. Since the Supreme Court's 1978 *Bakke* decision, schools have been allowed to consider race as a factor in college applications. The Texas case indicates that this practice might be ending.[4]

Similar lawsuits have occurred over the issue of minority scholarships, and the U.S. Supreme Court's decisions could ultimately change the standards American universities have been using to offer financial aid to minorities. By the mid-1990s, roughly two-thirds of U.S. universities were setting aside

The University of California at Berkeley recruited more minority students than most other top-level schools. The results, however, were questionable.

scholarship money exclusively for minority students.[5] This practice, too, may become a thing of the past.

The Benjamin Banneker Scholarship, given by the University of Maryland, is an example of a scholarship program under legal attack even though it gives scholarships based on *merit* as well as race. Created in 1979 as part of the school's efforts to conform to federal desegregation standards, the Banneker program, by almost all accounts, greatly enriched the campus and made it one of the most hospitable in the country to a diverse population. By recruiting outstanding African American students, the Banneker Scholarship created a perfect atmosphere for the rise of black campus leaders alongside their white counterparts. It also bridged the gaps between black students and white students.

The University of Maryland offers a scholarship based on merit as well as race.

The Maryland campus, like most others, has had racial tension between blacks and whites. But supporters of the Banneker Scholarship claim it dramatically reduced hostility and promoted racial understanding. Stereotypes began to disappear as white students came to see that their black counterparts were not inferior students. Corey Davis, a Banneker scholar from Teaneck, New Jersey, says that white students came "to know us—we put a face on the issue."[6]

Although campuses nationwide were forced to reexamine their affirmative action policies about admissions, scholarships, and hiring, the issue drew the most attention in California. Because it is huge and diverse, many national trends are launched in this state. California's colleges and universities are often cited—

by *both* sides of the debate—to illustrate exactly what the results of several decades of affirmative action have been.

The University of California at Berkeley is often said to be the model of affirmative action because it recruited and attracted a higher percentage of minority students than most other top-level academic institutions. How has this school fared as a result? According to D'Souza, the results have been disastrous. He claims that only 22 percent of Hispanics and 18 percent of blacks who were admitted to Berkeley through affirmative action programs in 1982 had graduated by 1987. For those blacks and Hispanics who were *not* admitted through preferential programs, however, the graduation rate was 42 percent and 55 percent respectively.[7]

D'Souza has probably become more well known than any other writer for his stand against affirmative action on campuses, but many people disagree with much of what he says. D'Souza offers an interesting reason for the low graduation rate among minorities who were given preferential treatment. The reason, he says, is "misplacement." When colleges lower admission standards in order to raise the number of African American and Hispanic students on campus, D'Souza says misplacement occurs. In other words, students attend colleges for which they don't actually qualify. The course work is too difficult, and the competition with other students is too intense. The result is academic struggle, battered self-esteem, and ultimately a high dropout rate.[8]

Writer Viet D. Dinh also opposes affirmative action. He says that the push to admit other minorities has closed many doors for Asian American students and created serious tension among the races at Berkeley. Vandalism of the African Student Center and graffiti on bathroom walls saying "nips go home" are among the evidence of this tension.

Included in Dinh's argument is the following:

> From a remedial perspective, denying such entitlements to Asian Americans in order to admit other minority students cannot be justified. Asian Americans have as valid a claim of racial victimization as other minorities. Just as Africans were brought to America as slaves, Chinese were dragged here as indentured laborers, working in inhumane conditions to build the railroads that became the lifeline of America. Official acts, such as the Chinese Exclusion Act of 1882 and the internment of Japanese Americans during World War II, illustrate the institutional racism that defined the history of Asians in America.[9]

Chang-Lin Tien, chancellor of the University of California at Berkeley, disagrees, however. He has written extensively to combat what he considers "common myths about affirmative action at Berkeley." First, he says, the academic quality at Berkeley has not declined as the student population has diversified. "Of the freshmen admitted to our campus," he writes, "95 percent continue to rank among the top 12.5 percent of the statewide high school graduates. More important, [based on test scores and other indications] our academic standards are higher than ever, and each entering class is more talented than the last."[10]

The second myth about Berkeley admissions, Tien says, is that "diversity is limited to race and ethnicity.

Chang-Lin Tien, chancellor at the University of California at Berkeley, defends the school's affirmative action policy and encourages diversity on campus.

But our new admissions policies also assure that our doors are open to low-income students, older students with special talents, and students from rural and urban areas alike."[11]

Another common myth is that a diverse student population, once admitted, does not succeed academically. At Berkeley, according to Tien, the percentage of those who graduate within five years leaped from only 50 percent during the 1940s and 1950s (when the overwhelming majority of students were white) to 60 percent in the 1970s, and to 70 percent in the 1980s and 1990s. Moreover, "the graduation rates for all ethnic groups have improved significantly."[12]

It was not only the controversy over what has occurred on California college campuses that caused the national debate on affirmative action to focus on that state in 1996. The California Civil Rights Initiative (CCRI) injected the issue into the most populous state's election year campaign. Appearing on the ballot in November 1996 as Proposition 209 to be voted on by all California voters, the initiative intended, once and for all, to end affirmative action as it had existed for more than 30 years.

CCRI was conceived by two college professors to bar the state's government and universities from using race, ethnicity, or gender for "discriminating against or granting preferential treatment to any individual or group." Sponsors of CCRI had originally tried to get it adopted by the state legislature. When that failed, they got the proposal on the 1996 ballot as a public referendum so that California voters could decide the issue. Since California plays such a crucial role in presidential elections, CCRI's sponsors were deliberately sending elected officials a clear message about the public's disenchantment with affirmative action.[13]

The man who led the push for the CCRI was not one of the "angry white men" most often pictured as strongly against affirmative action. Ward Connerly, an African American, collected one million signatures needed to get the initiative on the ballot. As a member of the University of California Board of Regents who fondly referred to the November 1996 showdown as "a racial Super Bowl," Connerly endured criticism that, at times, was quite personal. State senator Diane Watson told the *Los Angeles Times:* "He's married to a white woman. He wants to be white. He wants a colorless society. He has no ethnic pride."[14]

University of California regent Ward Connerly chaired the campaign for Proposition 209.

But Connerly sees the world differently. He worked hard to achieve success and also benefited from individual acts of kindness and encouragement from whites while growing up in Sacramento. Connerly simply believes that "… if you take people at face value and give them an opportunity, race is irrelevant."[15] He has also said, "The truth is that preferences at this point are not just reverse discrimination, they're degrading to people who accept them. They've got to go."[16]

Proposition 209 (CCRI) became one of the most hotly debated issues of 1996, and, as voters in California and across the nation became increasingly aware of the proposition, both sides grew stronger, more vocal, and more emotional. Supporters used the words of Martin Luther King Jr. defining his dream of a color-blind society (until King's angry widow forced them to stop); opponents used terrifying images of the Ku Klux Klan.

On election day, November 5, 1996, nearly 55 percent of California's voters approved the ballot initiative. In other words, the majority wanted to ban affirmative action policies. But, as stated by *Newsweek* reporter Ellis Cose, "No one ever expected affirmative action to succumb without a whimper. And if the Proposition 209 battle is any indication, death will be fought every inch of the way."[17]

The first battleground turned out to be a U.S. district court. Within a few weeks of election day, a federal judge temporarily blocked enforcement of the CCRI. Chief U.S. district judge Thelton Henderson said the groups that filed the lawsuit (including the American Civil Liberties Union [ACLU], the National Organization for Women [NOW], and the National Association

California voters approved Proposition 209 in the November 1996 election.

Governor Pete Wilson of California put his state at the forefront of the anti-affirmative action movement.

for the Advancement of Colored People [NAACP]) had "demonstrated a strong probability" of proving the proposition to be unconstitutional.[18] At the time of this writing, legal experts predicted a definitive ruling on Proposition 209 probably would not be made for another year or more.

Governor Pete Wilson, who strongly supported CCRI, made it clear that his state would continue to be at the forefront of the anti-affirmative action movement. Why? Because he feels that Californians face a unique challenge. As Wilson said in a speech in July 1995, "We [in California] live in the most diverse society the world has ever known. In Los Angeles alone, our schools teach children who speak more than eighty different languages. Early in the next century, no single ethnic group will constitute a majority of California's population. We'll be the nation's first minority-majority state. So we don't need sermons about tolerance and diversity. We're practicing it every day."

This business conference appears to represent a color-blind and gender-neutral society. Can affirmative action achieve this goal without ignoring merit?

THE FUTURE OF AFFIRMATIVE ACTION

Stories continue to unfold in the media: the white New Jersey school teacher who was fired so a black colleague could be retained for the sake of "diversity goals;" the white police officer who was repeatedly denied promotion while 43 officers with lower scores on the departmental exam and with less seniority were moved ahead of him in the name of affirmative action;[1] an 87-year-old black woman who bequeathed her sizable life savings to a scholarship fund for black students, leaving people to wonder about the outcry this would have created if recipients had been exclusively white.[2] The questions never seem to get answered, and the resentment continues to grow in many Americans.

Affirmative action is not a controversy that anyone expects to disappear suddenly. But the fact that the debate is becoming more and more open and that all the complexities of the issue are being addressed every day shows true progress. It is important to note that

A diverse group of high school students works together to complete a project.

Proposition 209 represents the first time the American people were asked or allowed to vote on affirmative action. Why did it take so long?

According to *U.S. News & World Report* columnist John Leo, a taboo has been created around the topic, among American citizens and certainly among politicians. "A mixture of white guilt and fear about being denounced for racism sustained the taboo for a remarkably long time," wrote Leo. But, he adds, "taboos maintain their strength only as long as they remain undiscussable. As soon as they are widely argued pro and con, which will now occur with great energy in California, the taboo disappears."[3]

Most people agree that affirmative action policies at least need to be closely examined and revised. The goal that is often stated is to be a color-blind and gender-neutral meritocracy—in other words, a system that rewards individual achievement rather than preferred group membership. But critics of such a goal point out that real merit is difficult, if not impossible, to measure. Can high school grades and standardized test scores, for example, really predict the performance of all college applicants? And abolishing affirmative action policies would not eliminate other common forms of favoritism that ignore merit.

One of the most frequently suggested changes to affirmative action is to provide programs based not on race or gender, but on economic need. Class-based programs, it is argued, would serve only the most disadvantaged Americans, and such programs would be color-blind. But this solution is not as simple as it may sound. A form of reverse discrimination would still occur, and there would still be "victims" who are "passed over" regardless of how well they qualified for the school or job. The same stigma would remain—both to oneself and to others—of having gotten a chance because of affirmative action rather than strictly on merit. And how, exactly, would policymakers define and compare "disadvantage?"[4]

Some proponents of affirmative action would like to see policies based on economic need—rather than on race or gender.

Other solutions are being discussed as America heads toward the 21st century. In African American communities, the strongest words and warnings are directed inward. Along with many black leaders, activists, and writers, *Washington Post* columnist William Raspberry applauds the civil rights movement for its successful fight against "the external enemies of black progress." Even if affirmative action ends, victims of discrimination will still have the law behind them. But it is time now, Raspberry declares, "for a full-scale movement against the internal enemies of black progress."[5] These include family disintegration, teen pregnancy, drugs, gangs, crime, unemployment, violence, and despair.

This approach is nothing new. Over a century ago, Booker T. Washington spoke about the challenge of "self-emancipation" facing black Americans. He wrote in his *Autobiography,* "It is a mistake to assume that one man can, in any true sense, give freedom to another. Freedom, in the larger and higher sense, every man must gain for himself."[6]

Whatever changes continue to occur in affirmative action, the best policies for schools and workplaces nationwide will somehow make sure opportunities are available to all people without lowering standards and expectations. Such policies will often mean giving disadvantaged individuals the extra training and attention they need to meet high standards of performance—even if such action is labeled "preferential" treatment. Above all, effective affirmative action means making a genuine effort to find the many individuals in this diverse nation who might be overlooked but who have the capacity to excel.

Resources to Contact

American Association for
   Affirmative Action
3905 Vincennes Road, No. 304
Indianapolis, IN 46268-3026
800-252-8952

Equal Employment Advisory Council
1015 15th Street NW
Suite 1220
Washington, DC 20005
202-789-8650

Equal Rights Advocates
1663 Mission Street
Suite 550
San Francisco, CA 94103
415-621-0672

National Association for the
   Advancement of Colored People
4805 Mt. Hope Drive
Baltimore, MD 21215
410-358-8900

National Council of Educational
   Opportunity Associations
1025 Vermont Avenue NW
Suite 1201
Washington, DC 20005
202-347-7430

Wider Opportunities for Women
1325 G Street NW
Lower Level
Washington, DC 20005
202-638-3143

Endnotes

CHAPTER 1. WHAT IS AFFIRMATIVE ACTION?

[1]Lino A. Graglia, "Affirmative Discrimination," *National Review*, July 5, 1993, 28.

[2]Nicolaus Mills, "Introduction: To Look Like America," *Debating Affirmative Action*, edited by Nicolaus Mills (New York: Delta, 1994), 3.

[3]Roger Wilkins, "Racism Has Its Privileges," *The Nation*, March 27, 1995, 409.

[4]Michael Kinsley, "The Spoils of Victimhood," *The New Yorker*, March 27, 1995, 68.

[5]Ibid., 69.

[6]Ibid.

[7]Randall Kennedy, "Persuasion and Distrust: The Affirmative Action Debate," *Debating Affirmative Action*, 54.

[8]Steven Roberts, "Affirmative Action on the Edge," *U.S. News & World Report*, February 13, 1995, 32.

[9]Howard Fineman, "Race and Rage," *Newsweek*, April 3, 1995, 25.

[10]John Leo, "Finally, the people vote on a taboo," *U.S. News & World Report*, March 4, 1996, 26.

[11]Lou Gelfand, "Avoiding Terminology Land Mines," Minneapolis *Star Tribune*, August 20, 1995.

[12]Ellis Cose, "Blinded by Color," *Newsweek*, September 25, 1995, 72.

[13]Mills, 29.

[14]Hendrik Hertzberg and Henry Louis Gates Jr., "The African-American Century," *The New Yorker*, April 29 & May 6, 1996, 10.

[15]Ibid.

[16]Gina Pera, "Teens and Race," *USA Weekend*, Special Report, August 18–20, 1995, 1.

[17]Ibid.

[18]Wilkins, 415.

[19]Tom Dunkel, "Affirmative Reaction," *Working Woman*, October 1995, 96.

[20]Roberts, 32.

[21]Dunkel, 43.

[22]Chang-Lin Tien, "Diversity and Excellence in Higher Education," *Debating Affirmative Action*, 239.

[23]Mills, 30.

[24]Ibid., 31.

[25]Shelby Steele, "A Negative Vote on Affirmative Action," *Debating Affirmative Action*, 41.

[26]Mills, 32.

[27]James P. Pinkerton, "Why Affirmative Action Won't Die," *Fortune*, November 13, 1995, 193.

[28]Roberts, 32.

[29]Dunkel, 41.

[30]Manning Marable, "Staying on the Path to Racial Equality," *The Affirmative Action Debate*, edited by George Curry, (Reading, Massachusetts: Addison-Wesley Publishing Co., 1996), 15.

CHAPTER 2. HOW DID WE GET HERE?

[1]Steven Yates, *Civil Wrongs: What Went Wrong with Affirmative Action* (San Francisco: ICS Press, 1994), xvii.

[2]Graglia, 26.

[3]Mills, 5.

[4]Ibid., 6.

[5]Ibid.

[6]Ibid., 7.

[7]Ibid., 9.

[8]Ibid., 11.

[9]Ibid., 12.

[10]Ibid., 13.

[11]Ibid., 27.

[12]Ibid., 19.

[13]Ibid., 25.

[14]Ibid., 1.

[15]Ibid., 26.

[16]Ibid., 28.

[17]Yates, xviii.

[18]Roberts, 38.

CHAPTER 3. RACIAL DISCRIMINATION

[1]Stanley Fish, "Reverse Racism or How the Pot Got to Call the Kettle Black," *The Atlantic Monthly*, 135.

[2]Ruben Navarette Jr., "If You Hadn't Been Mexican," *Debating Affirmative Action*, 132.

[3]Mark Whitaker, "Whites v. Blacks," *Newsweek*, October 16, 1995, 31.

[4]Jerelyn Eddings, "The Covert Color War," *U.S. News & World Report*, October 23, 1995, 41.

[5]Ibid., 44.

[6]Ibid., 41.

[7]Wilkins, 412.

[8]Ibid., 410.

[9]Ibid., 414.

[10]Ibid., 410.

[11]Ibid.

[12]Cose, 75.

[13]Hertzberg and Gates, 10.

[14]Pera, 6.

[15]Ibid., 8, 9.

[16]Ibid., 1.

[17]Ibid., 10.

[18]Charles Murray, "Affirmative Racism," *Debating Affirmative Action*, 192.

[19]Ibid., 194.

[20]Ibid., 207.

[21]Ibid., 206.

[22]Barbara van Look, "D'Souza's Voice," *Destiny Magazine,* January 1996, 43.

[23]Cose, 72.

[24]Ibid.

[25]William Raspberry, "Only Racists Could Cheer 'The End of Racism,'" Minneapolis *Star Tribune,* September 22, 1995.

[26]Joseph G. Conti, Ph.D. and Brad Stetson, Ph.D., "Racism: Does It Really Exist?" *Destiny Magazine,* January 1996, 50.

[27]Ibid.

[28]Ibid., 51.

[29]Tom Teepen, "It's No Time to Dump Affirmative Action," *St. Paul Pioneer Press,* June 16, 1996.

[30]Conti and Stetson, 53.

[31]Ibid.

[32]Cornel West, "Our Next Race Question," *Harper's* Magazine, April 1996, 55.

[33]Ibid., 59.

[34]Ibid.

[35]Ibid., 60.

[36]Jim Sleeper, "Affirmative Action's Outer Limits," *Debating Affirmative Action,* 312.

[37]Yates, 27–29.

[38]Sleeper, 312.

CHAPTER 4. GENDER DISCRIMINATION

[1]Dunkel, 40.

[2]Ibid., 41.

[3]Philip J. Trounstine, "Feminists Fear Affirmative Action Loss," *St. Paul Pioneer Press,* March 12, 1995.

[4]Ibid.

[5]Ibid.

[6]Ibid.

[7]Ibid.

[8]Dunkel, 40.

[9]Alice Kessler-Harris, "Feminism and Affirmative Action," *Debating Affirmative Action,* 70.

[10]Ibid.

[11]Ibid., 68.

[12]Ellen Goodman, "Opening the Work Door for Women," *Debating Affirmative Action,* 101.

[13]Ibid., 102.

[14]Peter T. Killborn, "Top Corporate Jobs Still Elude Most Minorities, Women," Minneapolis *Star Tribune,* March 16, 1995.

[15]Ibid.

[16]Ibid.

CHAPTER 5. CALIFORNIA AS A CASE STUDY

[1]Steve Berg, "California's Universities, Nation Rethink Race, Fairness," Minneapolis *Star Tribune,* April 2, 1996.

[2]Ibid.

[3]Ibid.

[4]S. C. Gwynne, "Undoing Diversity," *Time,* April 1, 1996, 54.

[5]Joseph P. Shapiro, "How Much Is Enough?" *U.S. News & World Report,* February 13, 1995, 39.

[6]Ibid.

[7]Dinesh D'Souza, "Sins of Admission," *Debating Affirmative Action,* 233.

[8]Ibid.

[9]Viet D. Dinh, "Multiracial Affirmative Action," *Debating Affirmative Action,* 285.

[10]Tien, 243.

[11]Ibid., 244.

[12]Ibid., 245.

[13]Arch Puddington, "Will Affirmative Action Survive?" *Commentary,* October 1995, 22.

[14]Mike Tharp, "Gearing up for a 'Racial Super Bowl,'" *U.S. News & World Report,* March 25, 1996, 22.

[15]Ibid.

[16]B. Drummond Ayres Jr., "Taking on Affirmative Action," Minneapolis *Star Tribune,* April 1, 1996.

[17]Ellis Cose, "After Affirmative Action," *Newsweek,* November 11, 1996, 43.

[18]Associated Press, "Judge Rules against Proposition 209," *St. Paul Pioneer Press,* November 28, 1996.

[19]Pete Wilson, "The Minority-Majority Society," *The Affirmative Action Debate,* 167.

CHAPTER 6. THE FUTURE OF AFFIRMATIVE ACTION

[1]Jeremy Rabkin, "Bewitched and Bewildered by a Debate That Won't End," *The American Spectator,* October 1996, 72.

[2]Michael Kinsley, "Generous Old Lady, or Reverse Racist?" *Time,* August 28, 1995, 76.

[3]Leo, 26.

[4]Kinsley, "The Spoils of Victimhood," 66.

[5]Mortimer Zuckerman, "Black America's Mirror Images," *U.S. News & World Report,* May 6, 1996, 76.

[6]Glenn C. Loury, "Performing without a Net," *The Affirmative Action Debate,* 62.

Glossary

apartheid: the government policy in South Africa that required people of different races to live separately. The word is often used to indicate separateness or segregation in general.

civil rights: the rights to personal liberty and equal opportunity established by several of the amendments to the Constitution of the United States; the social and political movement to end racial discrimination

discrimination: prejudicial outlook, action, or treatment

diversity: a goal for workplaces and educational facilities to include people in their population who represent many different races, backgrounds, beliefs, and perspectives

ethnicity: relating to a group of people's unity that is based on shared race, language, religion, or culture

integration: the act or process of incorporating individuals of different groups, such as races, into society as equals

meritocracy: a system that is based strictly on rewarding individual merit (excellence) or achievement, not showing preference based on group membership

prejudice: a preconceived judgment or opinion formed without just grounds or sufficient knowledge

quota: a numerical expectation or requirement. In the realm of affirmative action, quotas are fixed percentages of minorites or women to be hired by employers or admitted to schools to create a diverse population.

stereotype: a standardized mental picture that is held in common by members of a group and that represents an oversimplified opinion or prejudiced attitude toward members of another group

stigma: a mark of shame or discredit

Bibliography

Conti, Joseph G. and Brad Stetson. "Racism: Does It Really Exist?" *Destiny* Magazine, January 1996.

Cose, Ellis. "The Myth of Meritocracy." *Newsweek,* April 3, 1995.

_____. "Blinded by Color," *Newsweek,* September 25, 1995.

_____. "After Affirmative Action." *Newsweek,* November 11, 1996.

Curry, George E., ed. *The Affirmative Action Debate.* Reading, Massachusetts: Addison-Wesley Publishing Company, Inc., 1996.

Dunkel, Tom. "Affirmative Reaction." *Working Woman,* October 1995.

Eddings, Jerelyn. "The Covert Color War." *U.S. News & World Report,* October 23, 1995.

Fineman, Howard. "Race and Rage." *Newsweek,* April 3, 1995.

Fish, Stanley. "Reverse Racism or How the Pot Got to Call the Kettle Black." *The Atlantic Monthly,* November 1993.

Graglia, Lino A. "Affirmative Discrimination." *National Review,* July 5, 1993.

Gwynne, S. C. "Undoing Diversity." *Time,* April 1, 1996.

Hertzberg, Hendrik and Henry Louis Gates Jr. "The African-American Century." *The New Yorker,* April 29 and May 6, 1996.

Kinsley, Michael. "The Spoils of Victimhood." *The New Yorker,* March 27, 1995.

Leo, John. "Finally, the People Vote on a Taboo." *U.S. News & World Report,* March 4, 1996.

Meyerson, Adam. "Nixon's Ghost." *Policy Review,* Summer 1995.

Mills, Nicolaus, ed. *Debating Affirmative Action.* New York: Delta, 1994.

Pera, Gina. "Teens and Race." *USA Weekend,* August 18–20, 1995.

Pinkerton, James P. "Why Affirmative Action Won't Die." *Fortune,* November 13, 1995.

Puddington, Arch. "Will Affirmative Action Survive?" *Commentary,* October 1995.

Rabkin, Jeremy. "Bewitched and Bewildered by a Debate That Won't End." *The American Spectator,* October 1996.

Roberts, Steven V. "Affirmative Action on the Edge." *U.S. News & World Report,* February 13, 1995.

Samuelson, Robert J. "Affirmative Action as Theater." *Newsweek,* August 14, 1995.

Shapiro, Joseph P. "How Much Is Enough?" *U.S. News & World Report,* February 13, 1995.

Tharp, Mike. "Gearing up for a 'Racial Super Bowl.'" *U.S. News & World Report,* March 25, 1996.

Van Look, Barbara. "D'Souza's Voice." *Destiny* Magazine, January 1996.

West, Cornel. "Our Next Race Question." *Harper's* Magazine, April 1996.

Whitaker, Mark. "Whites v. Blacks." *Newsweek,* October 16, 1996.

Wilkins, Roger. "Racism Has Its Privileges." *The Nation,* March 27, 1995.

Yates, Steven. *Civil Wrongs.* San Francisco: The Institute for Contemporary Studies Press, 1994.

Zuckerman, Mortimer. "Black America's Mirror Images." *U.S. News & World Report,* May 6, 1996.

Index

About the Author

JoAnn Bren Guernsey has published three young adult novels and coauthored a mystery series dealing with environmental issues. Her recently published nonfiction books address topics such as teen pregnancy, rape, abortion, animal rights, and capital punishment. She is an active member of the Society of Children's Book Writers and Illustrators and a contributor to Lerner's Pro/Con and Achievers series.

Guernsey lives in St. Paul, Minnesota, with her two teenage daughters, who love to debate—with her and everyone else—the issues addressed in her books.

Photo Acknowledgments

AP/Wide World Photos, 91, 50 (bottom right); Archive Photos, 35; Birmingham Public Library, 26; Corbis-Bettmann, 31, 50 (upper left); © Steven Ferry, 21, 54; © Robert Fried, 17, 85, 92; © Ed Kashi, 24, 48, 75 (bottom), 96; © Richard B. Levine, 66 (both); Len Be Pas, 61; Reuters/Bettmann, 14, 80; Reuters/Corbis-Bettmann, 41, 42 (top); Reuters/str/Archive Photos, 93; © Frances M. Roberts, 15; © Ron Sherman, 57; Collection of the Supreme Court of the United States, 40; University of Maryland, 86; UPI/Bettmann, 37, 55, 98; UPI/Corbis-Bettmann, 19, 28, 30, 38, 42 (bottom), 76, 77, 89; Visuals Unlimited, 70 [© F. H.Kolwicz], 64 [© Mark E. Gibson], 6, 58, 60, 75 (top) [© Jeff Greenberg]; © Jim West, 10, 33, 46, 79.